CHARLES DICKENS

Contents

Written by Jim Eldridge

Charles Dickens

Charles Dickens was a writer who lived in England in the 1800s. He wrote over 20 novels, and in his books he created some very famous and well-known characters. He wrote about poor people, rich people, kind people and wicked people. Many of the characters were based on people he had met while he was growing up.

Charles Dickens writing at his desk

a London soup kitchen serving food to the poor in 1858

Charles Dickens was very interested in how people lived and how they behaved. He wrote about what life was like living in London at that time.

The Dickens family

Charles Dickens was born on
7 February 1812, in Portsmouth.
Charles's father, John Dickens, was
a **clerk** in the Navy Pay Office, and his job
was to pay **wages** to sailors on board
ships, and also to the workers on
the docks. The Dickens family moved
many times because of John Dickens's
job, usually to towns on the coast
where the navy ports were. Like many
families at this time, Charles's parents
had lots of children and Charles had
seven brothers and sisters.

Charles Dickens's
father, John

Charles Dickens's
mother, Catherine

Portsmouth in the 1800s

In the 19th century, people didn't own houses unless they were very rich – they **rented** them instead. John Dickens earned enough money to rent a whole house for his family, and have a maidservant live with them.

In 1822, when Charles was ten years old, John Dickens was **transferred** to London, and the family lived in a house in Camden Town.

In the 19th century, Camden Town was a village outside London surrounded by fields.

Charles's parents liked to have the best of everything: the best clothes, the best furniture – and the best food! If you didn't have much money you ate food like potatoes, cheese, bread and a thin porridge called gruel. If you did have money, you could pay for food like meat and fish.

John Dickens and his wife, Elizabeth, spent more money than they earned. Sometimes they had to sell pieces of furniture to pay their food bills. When that wasn't enough, Charles's parents told him he had to start work to earn some money.

In the early 19th century most children worked if they were from poor families. Some small boys as young as five years old worked as chimney sweeps, and climbed up the insides of chimneys to clean them. Others swept the streets. Many children worked in factories sewing sacks or making ropes. Children's jobs were hard and sometimes dangerous.

Charles was not from a poor family, so he'd never worked before – instead he'd gone to school. But as he was the eldest boy in the family he had to work now, so his parents found him a job in a shoe polish factory. He was only 12 years old.

children workin a brick facto

The shoe polish factory

The shoe polish factory, Warren's Blacking, was near the River Thames in London. For six days a week Charles worked from eight in the morning until six at night, sticking labels on pots of black shoe polish. The factory was a dark, dirty and crumbling building and Charles hated the work. He described the factory as "a crazy tumble-down old house, overrun with rats".

Charles was paid six shillings a week. Today, this is only 30 pence, but at the time this was enough money to buy food and pay for somewhere to sleep. Charles did not get to keep the money he earned – he had to give it all to his parents.

a street in London in the 1800s

As well as working for ten hours a day, Charles walked three miles to and from the factory. **Gas lamps** lit the streets in the centre of London, but there was no lighting on the country roads between London and Camden Town. Charles started his job in the winter, so he had to walk in the dark. The roads were thick with mud when it rained, and slippery and frozen when it was cold.

Prison!

Only a few days after Charles started work at
the shoe polish factory, his father, John Dickens,
was arrested because he couldn't pay his bills.
He was put in Marshalsea, a **debtors'** prison in
Southwark, London. At that time, it was common
for whole families to live in the prison until
the money had been paid. This is what happened
to the Dickens family.

Marshalsea Prison

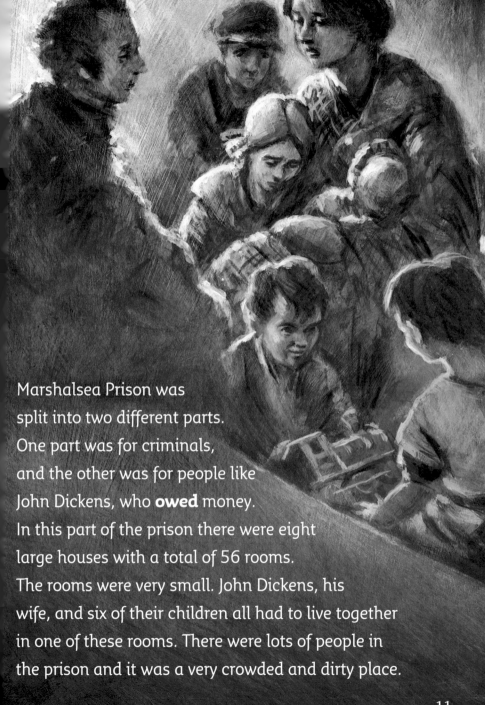

Marshalsea Prison was
split into two different parts.
One part was for criminals,
and the other was for people like
John Dickens, who **owed** money.
In this part of the prison there were eight
large houses with a total of 56 rooms.
The rooms were very small. John Dickens, his
wife, and six of their children all had to live together
in one of these rooms. There were lots of people in
the prison and it was a very crowded and dirty place.

The main gates of the prison were locked from
ten at night until eight in the morning. Half an hour
before the gates were locked, an officer walked around
the prison ringing a bell to tell visitors to leave.
If a visitor didn't get out in time, they had to spend
the night in prison.

Prisoners were not locked in their rooms. They could walk around the prison whenever they wanted, and they had to do their own cooking and cleaning.

Each **inmate** had to pay money to use the prison kitchen to boil water and cook meals.

Charles didn't live in the prison. He earned enough money from working at the factory to pay to live in one small room in a **lodging house** in Camden Town. He also had to pay for food for his family while they were in prison. On Sundays he went to the prison to see his family, but he did not like going there. He described the prison as slimy and rotten.

Freedom – but not for Charles

After a couple of months, John Dickens **inherited** some money and he paid his bills. Charles's parents couldn't afford to rent a whole house any more, so when the family left prison they moved into the same lodging house as Charles. Other people shared the house too, and the Dickens family lived in a few rooms. This was a much smaller space than they had lived in before, but bigger than the room at the prison. Charles, who'd had a room of his own, was now sharing with his parents and brothers and sisters.

When John Dickens was sent to prison he **retired** from his job. He was given a **pension**, but this was not enough money for the whole family to live on, so Charles had to keep working at the shoe polish factory. Charles didn't want to go back. When he was older he wrote: "I can never forget or forgive that my mother made me go back to the blacking factory."

School

When Charles was 13 he left the factory and went back to school. In the early 19th century children didn't have to go to school. If you did go, you had to pay. John Dickens had some money left from his inheritance after he'd paid his bills and he could now afford to send Charles to school again. John Dickens wanted Charles to be educated and become a gentleman but Charles didn't like the school, and he thought the teaching was terrible; he described the head teacher as "the most **ignorant** man I have ever known".

There were over 200 boys at the school. They sat in rows on wooden benches with wooden desks. Paper was very expensive so children used to write by scratching on a piece of **slate**.

The teachers were very **strict**, and if a boy didn't behave he could be hit with a stick. After two years, John Dickens ran out of money once more. Charles was 15 years old when he had to leave school again and go back to work.

In Victorian schools the classes were large, and pupils sat in rows.

Charles becomes a law clerk

Charles could read and write, so he got a job as a **law clerk** at a **law firm** in London. He had to copy out **wills**, and take papers to and from other law firms in London, and the law courts.

Victorian law courts were busy and noisy.

Victorian London was a dirty
and smelly place.

Charles walked everywhere, but in the 19th century
London was smelly, dirty and dangerous. The streets were
always covered with horse dung from all the horse-drawn
vehicles and many people got knocked down by carriages.

There was also the danger of smog. This was a mixture of
smoke, which came from coal fires and factories,
and fog. Londoners called smog a "pea-souper"
because it was thick and green – like pea soup.
Sometimes the smog was so thick even the light from
the gas lamps couldn't be seen.

Charles the writer

Charles wasn't interested in the law, but he was interested in the people he saw in court – the criminals and the victims of crime. When he was 18, Charles became a reporter. He went to the law courts and wrote about what happened there.

When Charles was 21 years old, his first short story was published. He didn't get paid for it, but it helped to get him known as a writer. He also wrote for a newspaper about what London life was like.

Charles wrote for a London newspaper called the *Evening Chronicle*.

Charles's first full-length book was published in 1836, when he was 24 years old. This time he was paid – £100. It would have taken Charles over three and a half years to earn the same amount of money working as a law clerk, and he now had enough money to move out of the rooms he lived in with his parents and brothers and sisters, and live on his own.

Charles's first book

Charles Dickens's family

In 1836, Charles married a young girl
called Catherine. By this time, he
was earning a lot of money as
a writer and he and his wife
could afford to rent a whole
house in a good area of
London called Bloomsbury.

Charles and Catherine had
ten children. With a large
family to support, Charles
needed most of the money he
earned, but he always gave money
to his parents, brothers and sisters.

Catherine Dickens

In the 19th century there was no television or radio
and families entertained themselves by reading
to one another, or playing the piano and singing.
Charles and Catherine had enough money
to see plays at the theatre and go to music concerts.
This was very different from Charles's life
at the shoe polish factory.

Charles reading to his daughters, Mary and Kate

Travel

By 1841, Charles was a very famous writer, even though he was only 29. He had published many books, which had sold thousands of copies. His stories weren't just **popular** in Britain. American readers loved them too, so his American publishers invited him to tour the country, reading his stories to audiences.

In January 1842, Charles and Catherine went to America. Aircraft had not been invented then, so it took a long time to get from Europe to America. Charles and Catherine's journey across the Atlantic was made in the small steamship *Britannia*, which took 17 days. It was rough for a large part of the journey; the seas in the Atlantic in January were wild and stormy. But it was worth it.

the steamship *Britannia*

Charles was one of the first English writers to travel to America on a reading tour, and he was a huge success.

Charles went on many reading tours around Britain too, and he often went by train. In June 1865, the train he was travelling in crashed off the rails. Charles helped the injured passengers before others arrived. Just before he left the crash, he remembered he had left the manuscript of his latest book in the carriage and ran back to get it.

a painting of Charles Dickens at a reading of one of his books

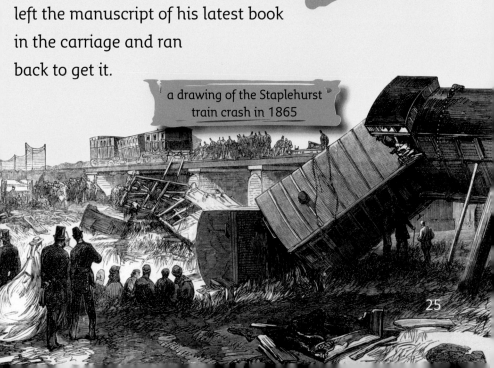

a drawing of the Staplehurst train crash in 1865

Charles made his last public appearance on 2 May 1870, at a reading in London attended by the Prince of Wales (later King Edward VII). On 8 June, Charles had a heart attack and he died the next day. The book he was writing at the time was never finished. He was 58 years old. Charles was buried in Poets' Corner in Westminster Abbey. This was a very special honour: only the greatest writers like William Shakespeare are buried there.

Poets' Corner, Westminster Abbey

CHARLES DICKE
BORN 7TH FEBRUARY 181
DIED 9TH JUNE 1870

Charles Dickens today

Many people think that Charles Dickens is the greatest writer of stories who ever lived. Charles had been poor and he'd been rich, and when he wrote about what life was really like for people – especially children – in the 19th century, he was writing about his own life and the people he met.

His books are still read today, 200 years later.

Dickens's books have also inspired successful films, plays and musicals.

Glossary

clerk	someone who writes records and copies information, in an office
debtors	people who owe money
gas lamps	lamps that get their light from a gas flame rather than electricity
ignorant	not knowing very much
inherited	received something from someone who had died
inmate	someone who is locked up in a prison
law clerk	someone who keeps records in a lawyers' office
law firm	a company that deals with matters to do with the law
lodging house	a house where people can rent rooms to live in
owed	had to pay back money to someone
pension	money paid regularly to someone when they are too old to work
popular	liked by a lot of people
rented	paid to use something which was owned by someone else
retired	stopped work because of old age
slate	a smooth, hard, thin piece of rock
strict	very keen to make people stick to the rules
transferred	moved
wages	payments to someone in return for their work
wills	documents in which people write down what should happen to their money after they die

Index

The life of a writer

1825: Charles goes back to school.

1812: Charles Dickens is born in Portsmouth.

1830: Charles becomes a reporter.

1810   1820   1830

1824: Charles starts work at the shoe polish factory.

1827: Charles becomes a law clerk.

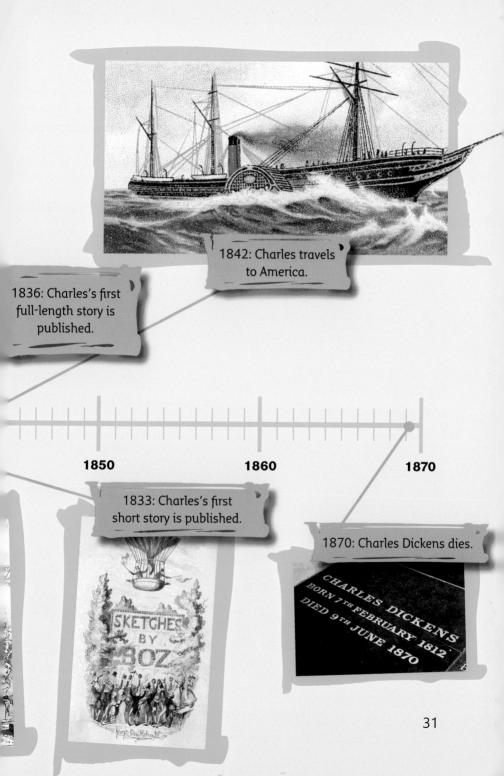

1842: Charles travels to America.

1836: Charles's first full-length story is published.

1850

1860

1870

1833: Charles's first short story is published.

1870: Charles Dickens dies.

SKETCHES BY BOZ

CHARLES DICKENS
BORN 7TH FEBRUARY 1812.
DIED 9TH JUNE 1870

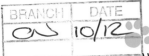

Ideas for reading

Written by Clare Dowdall BA(Ed), MA(Ed)
Lecturer and Primary Literacy Consultant

Learning objectives: read independently and with increasing fluency longer and less familiar texts; explain organizational features of texts including alphabetical order, layout, diagrams, captions, and bullet points; speak with clarity and use appropriate intonation when reading and reciting from texts; adopt appropriate roles in small or large groups and consider alternative courses of action

Curriculum links: History

Interest words: biography, century, clerk, novel, wages, transferred, rented, maidservant, gruel, chimney sweep, shillings, gas lamps, debtor, inmate, lodging house, inherited, retired, pension, ignorant, slate

Word count: 2,111

Resources: whiteboard, books by Charles Dickens, internet

Getting started

- Ask children if they have heard of the famous Victorian writer, Charles Dickens. Explain that they will be reading a biography, which tells us about his life and is written by another author.

- Look at the illustration of Charles Dickens on the front cover and read the blurb together. Establish that Charles Dickens is one of the greatest writers of all time, and discuss what this means.

- Discuss what the children know about life in the 19th century and make notes of their ideas on the whiteboard.

Reading and responding

- Read pp2–4 together to begin to find out about Charles Dickens. Discuss the content of the pictures and how life might have been in Dickens' time, e.g. the streets were crowded; the men wore tall hats.

- Model reading pp4–5, collecting as many facts as possible using a spider chart with Charles Dickens' name at the centre.